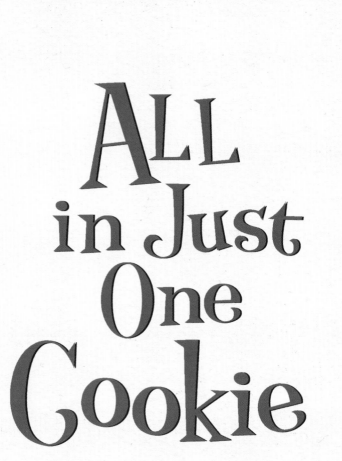

All in Just One Cookie

BY Susan E. Goodman

ILLUSTRATED BY Timothy Bush

Greenwillow Books
An Imprint of HarperCollinsPublishers

"They're on their way. I've got to get cookin'," says Grandma, hanging up the phone.

The butter is already out waiting. Grandma stoops and stretches to gather the rest of the ingredients for chocolate chip cookies.

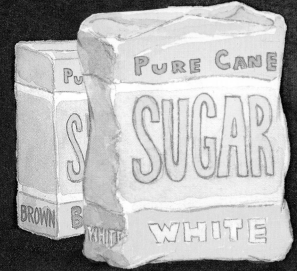

READY...
Check the recipe... Wash my hands...
Gotta go to the library!
Gotta log on to the internet!
Paper!
Pencils!
Grandma's encyclopedias!
So much work. I'm gonna need a snack.
SET...

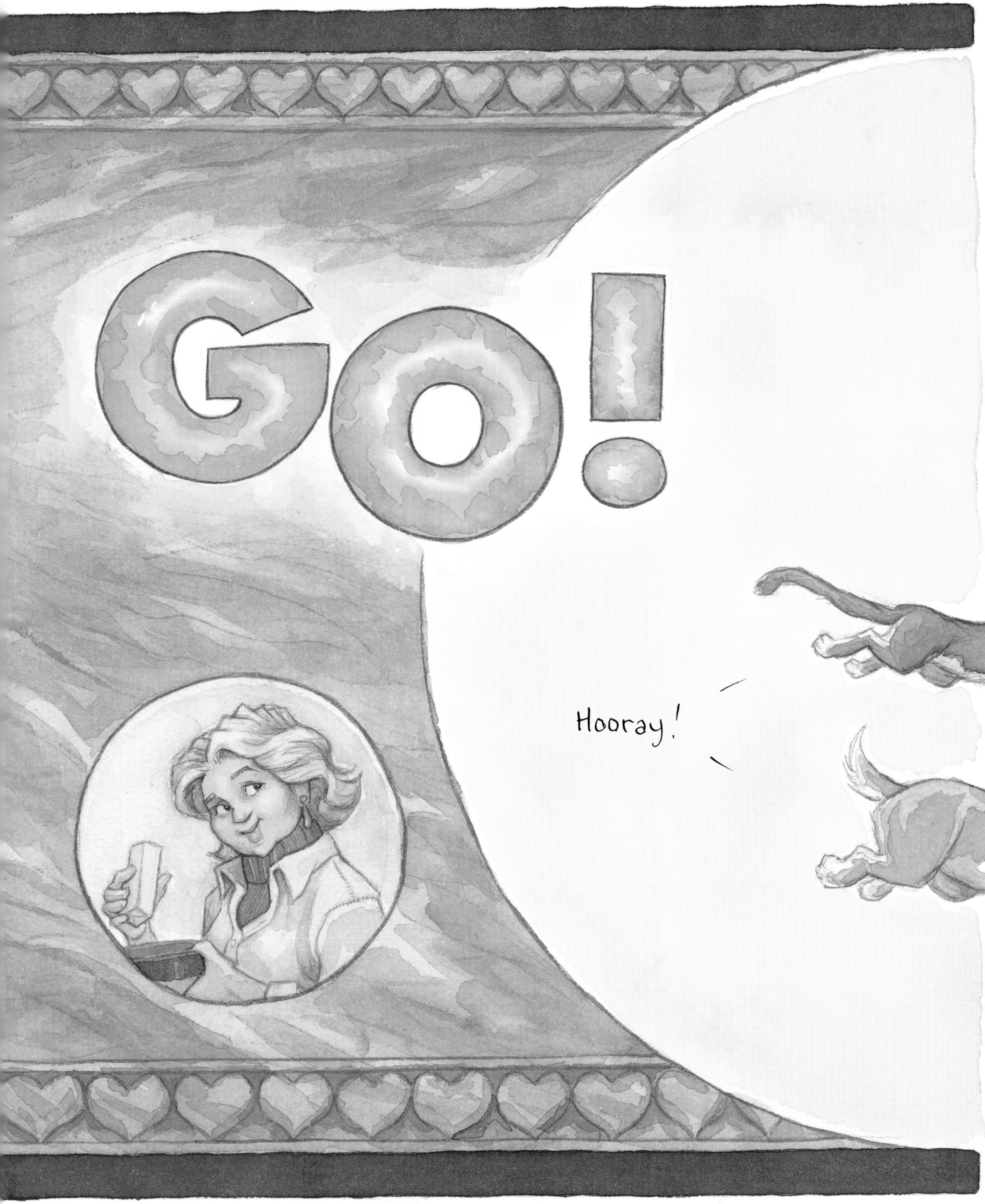
GO!
Hooray!

Butter

"Plop one," says Grandma as the first stick of softened butter drops into the mixing bowl.

"And plop two!"

Butter starts with a hungry Vermont cow eating the grass and grain that help her make milk. A dairy cow can produce almost 50 pounds of the stuff a day. It takes 21 pounds of milk to make a pound of butter.

Nowadays, farmers use machines to milk cows. Another machine then spins the milk around so fast that it comes apart. The heavier liquid flows outward. The lighter cream is pushed to the center, then up and out . . .

It says here that cows have four stomachs.

I wish I had four stomachs! I could eat four times more.

BUTTER
Spread the Word

. . . to the churn, which swirls the cream into a crashing sea of milky foam. After a lot of slosh and jiggle, a grain of butter appears, then another and another. Soon all of these grains get pushed along to be washed and drained.

Pressed into shape, wrapped in paper, the butter is ready to sell.

SUGAR!

Grandma pours in three-quarters of a cup of white sugar.

Then she packs a measuring cup three-quarters full of brown sugar. When she turns it upside down, a soft brown pyramid falls into the bowl.

500 years ago, sugar was called "white gold" because it was so expensive.

White gold? That's what I call my bones!

In Hawaii, sugarcane grows twenty feet high in fields as thick as jungles. Sugarcane is a grass, but one with stalks up to three inches across.

At the mill, huge rollers squeeze the chopped cane. They produce a waterfall of juice that is boiled into ever thicker, ever sweeter brown syrup.

Just as the last liquid boils away, a few sugar crystals are added. And the sugar in the syrup plays follow the leader. One speck after another changes into brown crystals, or raw sugar.

To become white sugar, these crystals get a shower that washes away their golden coat of molasses. But this cleaning turns them back into syrup so that water must, once more, be boiled away. Again, added sugar crystals help the rest grow into crystals— this time, sugar white.

Brown sugar gets a shorter shower so it keeps some of its molasses coating—and some of its deep flavor. Like white sugar, this dark brown syrup boils back into crystals. Slightly soft, slightly sticky, the brown sugar is packed into airtight plastic. That way it stays moist until Grandma uses it.

Two stalks of cane make just about the right amount of sugar for a batch of chocolate chip cookies.

Eating sugar gives you energy.

And I think YOU'VE had enough.

Wheeee!

Yikes!

Well, I see why they do all that stuff to it...

Mmmmmm.

A luscious smell drifts through the kitchen as Grandma drizzles a teaspoon of vanilla into the bowl.

Vanilla

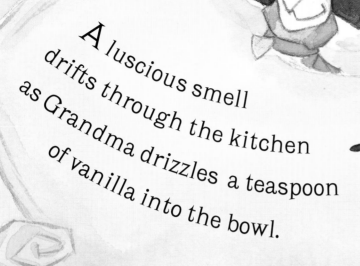

A new flower blooms on the vanilla vine—and the race is on. This tiny orchid stays open for less than a day and must be pollinated to produce its seeds.

AFRICA

MADAGASCAR

Farmers could transplant vanilla vines to Madagascar, but not the little Mexican bees that visit each flower and spread its pollen.

HAND POLLINATION

So farmers do the job themselves.

ACTUAL SIZE

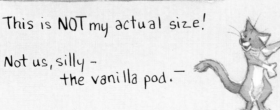

— This is NOT my actual size!

Not us, silly — the vanilla pod. —

"Better than perfume," she declares, putting a dab behind each ear.
She beats the ingredients until they're creamy.

Mmmmmm.

GROWING PODS

The seedpods grow longer and longer. Each is picked as soon as the first streak of yellow colors its tip.

Drying makes pods shrink.
DRYING PODS

The pods ripen by soaking up the morning sun and resting in an airtight box at night.

BUNDLED PODS

Then they are bundled . . .

. . . and sent to a factory to be chopped into pieces. A liquid is poured over them again and again until it takes on their scent and savor. This extract will bring vanilla's rich taste to ice cream, cakes, and chocolate chip cookies.

I'm glad I don't have to take that many baths!

Maybe you'd smell this good if you did!

PURE VANILLA EXTRACT

Eggs

Grandma cracks one egg into the bowl, and then another.

Done yet?

Not yet...

This time she beats the mixture until it's light and fluffy.

Thirty minutes after laying her last egg, a hen in New Hampshire starts making another one. It takes just a few hours to form the insides, then twenty more to make the shell.

About a day later, between 5 and 11 A.M., she picks her favorite nest. It has red curtains around it. Hens like their privacy.

Her egg rolls onto a moving conveyor belt underneath the nest. It joins thousands of others traveling this egg highway out of the giant barn and through a tunnel to another building.

They stream through a "car wash" for eggs that spins them and cleans them with warm water and brushes.

The eggs pass over strong lights so people can see inside. Workers remove the "crackeds" and "dirties," making sure the rest are perfect, Grade AA.

Weighed and sorted into sizes, the eggs gently roll to their packing stations, where they are put into cartons. Long before a day has passed, the eggs are in a refrigerated truck heading toward a supermarket.

Salt

Grandma spills a bit of salt when she pours it into the teaspoon measure.

Grandma isn't superstitious—not really—but she tosses a pinch over her left shoulder.

Grandma's salt comes from the Pacific Ocean. Water is pumped into shallow ponds near San Francisco. There, sun and wind start evaporating the water, coaxing it into the air.

As the remaining water gets saltier, it's pumped into other ponds. Little creatures living in them turn the ponds into a rainbow of low-salt greens, saltier oranges, and saltiest scarlets.

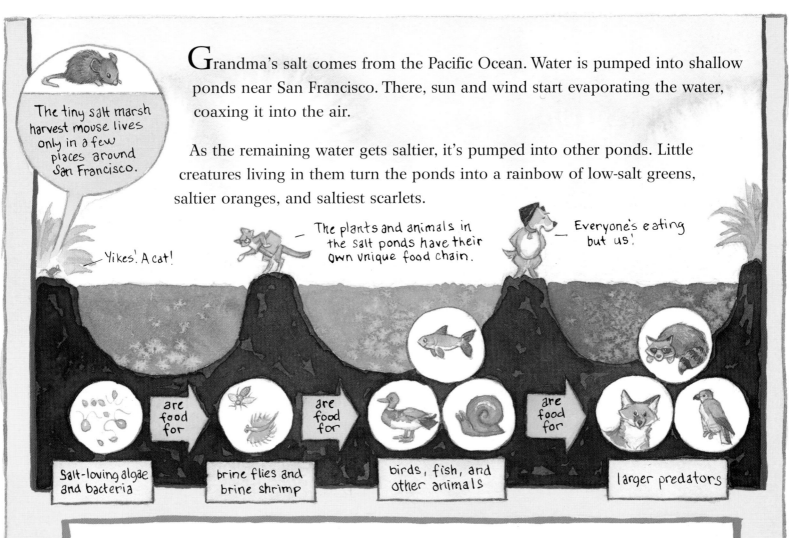

The tiny salt marsh harvest mouse lives only in a few places around San Francisco.

Yikes! A cat!

The plants and animals in the salt ponds have their own unique food chain.

Everyone's eating but us!

Salt-loving algae and bacteria

are food for

brine flies and brine shrimp

are food for

birds, fish, and other animals

are food for

larger predators

Eventually, the water contains as much salt as it can hold. When more water evaporates, the extra salt is forced to leave and drops to the bottom of the pond as solid crystals. At the end of the season, before winter rains reclaim the salt, farmers scrape up their harvest.

In many places, salt is still harvested by hand.

THE ROCK WE EAT

But not here! Out of the way, down there!

At the factory, the salt is washed with water so salty the crystals can't dissolve into it. This time, a machine evaporates the extra water away.

Sifting sorts the crystals into different sizes, including the one for saltshakers and chocolate chip cookies.

Baking Soda

Baking soda helps make cookies and cakes rise.

If I ate enough of it, would I get any taller?

Fifty million years ago, a huge lake sparkled in steamy sunshine. Over time, its water dried up. Layers of rock and dirt covered the lake bed.

Today, this spot is a desert in Wyoming. Deep in the ground, miners use huge machines with twirling spikes to break into walls of trona, a mineral the lake left behind. Conveyor belts send the chunks back through miles of tunnels to be hoisted above.

Fossilized BONES!

I think after 50 million years, they're too old even for... Hey! Are those FISH bones?

Grandma scrapes a knife over the top of the measuring spoon so she can add a level teaspoon of baking soda.

Crushed then baked, washed then dried, the mineral travels by train to the baking soda factory. There, it is dumped into a tank as big as a house, mixed with hot water and carbon dioxide gas, and . . . *poof!* Chemical magic creates baking soda crystals.

Once dried, the baking soda is boxed and ready to be measured, teaspoon by teaspoon, into chocolate chip cookies. Without it, Grandma's cookies would be pale and heavy.

This trona is amazing. It's used to make glass and soap and paper and...

COOKIES!

I LOVE this machine!

SODA
Pop and
Fizzle

Flour

Next comes the flour—
two and one-quarter cups.

It used to take farmers in Kansas a day to harvest an acre of wheat by hand. Now a combine gobbles two acres' worth every hour. It cuts the wheat and separates out the seeds, or kernels, and pours them into a truck driving alongside.

At the mill, flour making begins by cleaning these kernels. Millers vacuum them and pass them over magnets to remove dirt and straw, stones, and bits of metal.

Grandma adds and blends, making sure each speck of white disappears into the mix. When the last of the flour hits the whirring beaters, a cloud puffs out of the bowl.

Toothy rollers crush the kernels just enough to crack their outside covers and grind part of what's within.

Jiggled through a stack of sifters, only the finest powder can make it to the bottom. The miller will grind the remaining chunks to make other types of flours. But this first, purest flour is what goes into Grandma's chocolate chip cookies.

One bushel of wheat makes enough flour for 75 batches of chocolate chip cookies.

FLOUR POWER

Better tell Grandma to keep the oven on!

CHOCOLATE

Joy!

Joy!

As Grandma sprinkles two cups of chocolate chips onto the dough, a few fall on the counter. "What a delicious pity!" says Grandma, popping them into her mouth.

Around the world—in West Africa, Indonesia, Ecuador, and the Dominican Republic—the pods on cocoa trees grow to the size of footballs. When they're ripe, workers split them open with machetes. The beans inside are cream-colored, not brown, and taste bitter, not sweet at all.

Off to an American factory where the beans are roasted luscious brown. A machine cracks them open and gets their meat, or nibs, ready to crush into thick paste.

Cocoa trees bloom year-round, so flowers, growing pods, and ripe fruit can all be on the same tree at the same time.

Raw

Roasted

Then presses push all the liquid out of this goo until the remaining cakes of cocoa powder resemble the wheels of a railroad train.

These "wheels" squeeze through giant rollers that mix them with cocoa butter, sugar, and vanilla. Then another machine stirs the chocolate for hours, even days, until it is exactly right.

Finally, dollops of hardening chocolate are ready for their starring role in chocolate chip cookies.

Baking

Mounds of dough line each cookie sheet. Grandma slides them into the hot oven and sets the timer.

In the oven, three hundred seventy-five degrees of heat starts changing the dough. The butter and sugar melt quickly and the mounds begin to spread.

But they are rising, too. Air, trapped inside the eggs when they were beaten, swells in the hot oven. Bubbles from the baking soda and steam from the melting butter lift the dough some more.

The mounds rise and spread—but not for long. The heat is also cooking the eggs and flour. Together, they harden the mounds into their final shape. Then the sugar and baking soda turn them an inviting golden brown.

In about ten minutes, the heat has done its job. The ingredients have become something new . . . chocolate chip cookies, ready to come out of the oven.

A world of ingredients has gone into each of Grandma's cookies.

Atlantic Ocean

Europe

Asia

Africa

Indian Ocean

CHOCOLATE
Indonesia

CHOCOLATE
West Africa

VANILLA
Madagascar

Australia

The cookies are out and cooling when the doorbell chimes.

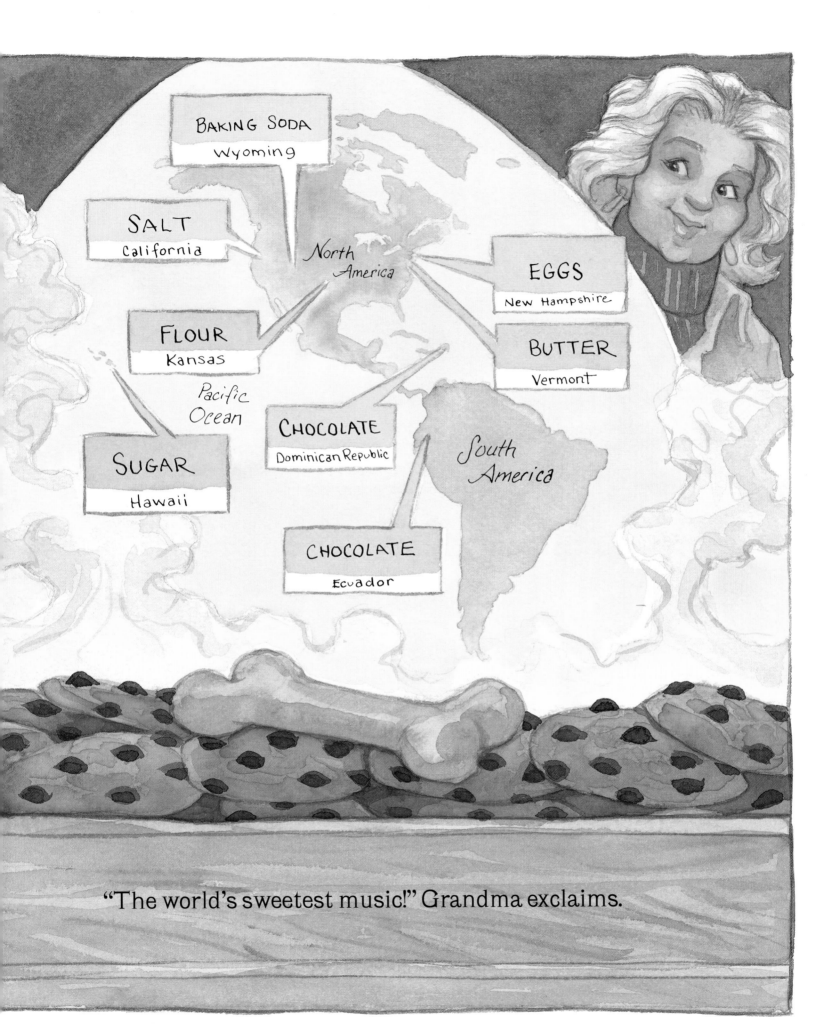

"The world's sweetest music!" Grandma exclaims.

CHOCOLATE CHIP COOKIES

2 sticks softened butter
¾ cup white sugar
¾ cup firmly packed brown sugar
1 teaspoon vanilla extract
2 eggs

1 teaspoon salt
1 teaspoon baking soda
2¼ cups flour
2 cups chocolate chips

Preheat the oven to 375° F.

Combine the butter, white sugar, brown sugar, and vanilla extract in a large bowl.
Mix well. Add eggs and beat until creamy. Stir in the salt and baking soda.
Gradually add the flour. Stir in the chocolate chips.

Drop rounded tablespoons of batter onto an ungreased cookie sheet.

Bake for 9–11 minutes, or until the cookies start to brown around their edges.
Transfer to cooling racks.

Makes 4 dozen cookies.

A note from the author: *All in Just One Cookie* depicts the story of Grandma's ingredients. Luckily, many areas produce the ingredients for chocolate chip cookies. You could write a geographic ABC book using the names of places where wheat flour is grown, for example. Several tropical countries are home to cocoa trees and vanilla orchids. And eggs are found wherever there are chickens.

To the people at Greenwillow—Virginia, Chad and Sylvie, Tim, Lois, Paul, Colleen, and especially Rebecca—who lovingly treat each book as if it were their own—S. E. G.

All in Just One Cookie. Text copyright © 2006 by Susan E. Goodman. Illustrations copyright © 2006 by Timothy Bush. All rights reserved.
Manufactured in China. www.harperchildrens.com Watercolors were used to prepare the full color art. The text type is Wilke Roman.
Library of Congress Cataloging-in-Publication Data: Goodman, Susan E., (date).
All in just one cookie / by Susan E. Goodman; pictures by Timothy Bush.   p.   cm. "Greenwillow Books." ISBN-10: 0-06-009092-8 (trade bdg.)
ISBN-13: 978-0-06-009092-0 (trade bdg.) ISBN-10: 0-06-009093-6 (lib. bdg.) ISBN-13: 978-0-06-009093-7 (lib. bdg.)
1. Cookies—Juvenile literature. 2. Baking—Juvenile literature. I. Bush, Timothy. II. Title.   TX772.G65 2005 641.8'654—dc22 2005030408
First Edition 10 9 8 7 6 5 4 3 2 1    Greenwillow Books